KILLING

IT

KILLING IT

POEMS

—

GAIA RAJAN

BLACK LAWRENCE PRESS

Black
Lawrence
Press

www.blacklawrence.com

Executive Editor: Diane Goettel
Chapbook Editor: Kit Frick
Book and Cover Design: Zoe Norvell

Cover Art: "cinéma du corps" by Saniya Singh. Used with permission.
Copyright © Gaia Rajan 2022
ISBN: 978-1-62557-046-8

TABLE OF CONTENTS

———

KILLING IT

My folks say hoping's good but it'll never save you,
because in our Ohio the best you'll get is broke
televangelists and ravenous churches. My folks
are bootstrap royalty. Crisp in cuffed shirts and gold
wedding rings that flash on a backhand slap. I was the prodigal
daughter and then a prodigy, the child mothers prayed for,
spelling bee queen, good at silence. In town they say we don't
deserve our breath but we call ourselves holy anyway
because even gods have short memories. All my friends are bored
waitress girls who fold tips in their skirts like scriptures
and touch up smudged lipstick at the altar of convenience
store bathrooms. We line our cheeks with drive-through
grease and never talk about our bodies. Wait in the backseat
for a damp god. Like all good disciples, we are grateful
for our unmaking. We neon we bleeding leaving
one by one for the redeye shift. My folks believe
in lotteries, not failures. The opposite of dead
is exemplary. They believe this every time they abandon me
kneeling at their beauty, their model, their myth. My folks know all
that is holy is only a failure of distance; white man,
far enough away, turns to god. Sometimes
when people say I'm killing it I remember everything
exemplary I know or ever will traces back to a small girl
on the floor praying *please, please, can you save me*

OHIO

At fifteen, you're not freckled, not blushing, not brave
enough to scale the fence or let your mother see you
love a girl, so you hold out for senior year in the arcade,
where the worlds before ours ended, you play pinball
with a girl who could've loved you and feel
like a murderer, take this fear into your hips,
your hands, your name, hide it in your bedroom
where you chew the ballpoint pen
you borrowed from the science fair you lost
in second grade as you listen to success stories
of conversion therapy in New York.
You barely remember when your mother
found a poem you'd hidden in your backpack
about a girl at school and left the lights on
for four nights straight, looking at you
like you were monstrous or dead, and finally,
you drove together through highways in silence
and she put the radio on and you skipped
the station whenever you heard a curse word,
and when you pulled back into the driveway she said,
quietly, *you are not one of them.* All you remember
is when you were six and she taught you
how to swim, and you were so good at it,
you barely needed lessons, until she took you
to real water, the currents forcing you down
and down, you helpless and clawing for air
in Ohio's deepest lake, the same way you gasped crying

on a park bench, harder when a stranger promised
it always gets better, neither of you believing it.

BEARINGS

*In the myth of Thessalonike, a young girl walks
into the sea after her brother's death, intending to
die, but becomes a mermaid instead.*

By then I could hear water everywhere—in the walls,
in my knees, under the stone slabs of my bathroom,

in my lover's arched ear. My hair never dried.
I kissed her, tasted salt. Once again I resolved to live

needing less. Peeled each wrinkle
from my fingers and didn't wince. At night,

I practiced holding my breath, standing in rain,
water flinching from my boots. Alone

in the dark, I yelled my lover's name, voice blurry
and blooming like some primordial squid. I was free

to love anything I wanted, though I didn't
love her. Though every night next to her I dreamt myself

something terrible—viperfish, lamprey, mutant
shark—and I broke the surface, fled back

to my dark ooze of a body, praying by morning
she wouldn't remember my older, softer skin

HEAVEN

Once, there was only flesh eating flesh eating flesh. Efficient. Once,
a taxonomist wanted to know if women were engineered to perform
labor, so he exhumed teeth, sewed them into a girl. In an empty room,

I watched a rocket stall, then take off elsewhere. The taxonomist
sent his daughter to the factories, and she worked until
her fingers rotted, until her jaws unhinged

to reveal radioactive cogs, and she opened
and opened and opened. A matter of willpower: the creatures
evolved teeth, wrapped their jaws around the necks

of prey, bit down and did not draw sound. The daughter glistened
and once again became useful. We clutched her bones like lanterns
and bounced light off the walls of the factory. I applauded

the rocket's extraordinary progress, alone in the dark,
watching the machinery's steel grow like a wound and open
and open. The taxonomist plucked out my eyes to understand

my negative thoughts. His daughter screamed
in her narrow house, grew a second spine, a new mouth.
The creatures killed their ancestors with efficient guns;

they lasted through the difficult winter. I knelt
at the blood of my better selves, selves I killed
with my bare beautiful hands,

and wept. The taxonomist named the experiment
a success. He opened his daughter, and found so much
husk, so little blood, you wouldn't believe.

SIMPLE MACHINES

At eleven, I stole a lisp from my parents—slipped
past silent seams of brick, past slouching yards

and surveilling fields, past the stray dog still wearing
its owner's collar, past the trappings of dead

animals and the splintering lanterns in perfect
hunting lodges, past the people and their economies

of sweat and the gym called Manifest Your Destiny
into the speech classroom's projector spotlight. There's more steel

in English than you would believe. In my textbooks,
men invented new machines to turn people

into ghosts, to sheathe our senses in fresh
blood. The woman in speech class asked all

who hadn't broken their mouths yet to circle
the nouns. Mark the verbs. Buck the horse. Stolen

accent evidence of stagnancy. A cycle
of innovation: pulley into crank into guillotine.

The inventions grew more beautiful, more
deadly: artful casket, gorgeous cage. I learned

how to speak so they could ruin me, an imitation
of a voice. All of this is progress. I excelled

in speech class, my mouth rinsed clean with white
heat, controlled vocabularies of so much blood. On days

I can't speak, this is where I go: interrogation
room, gunmetal smile. Grateful machines. The coldest tongues.

PRODIGY

They tilled the fields after the best harvest yet
and dredged the dead bodies up. *Channel the fear,*

       the orchestra conductor screamed: we learned Bach,
       left the stage to plunge our fingers

into the dark. We played a restaurant where, four years ago,
a man bludgeoned his wife and fled

       to Iowa. The dogs found the wife—an oak shoved her
       into the yard. The concertmaster Alice hid from her voice

in the corn, escaped her ghosts and the living
corpses of this town until she ran,

       bleeding, white-hot, into herself—
       gone. The murderer's wife was blue-haired and

Asian and beautiful and pregnant and seventeen.
I sat in the back of the orchestra

       and played harmony, Alice's lipstick still smeared
       on my teeth. No one could hear me

when I wept in my mother's house. The light burst
through the window and tried

to slit my throat. They found another corpse in the fields
and I dreamt of running, changing my name to Awe

and shearing off my hair with a butcher knife,
asking for mercy on a highway. Cue the violins.

I auditioned for concertmaster, failed again.
Played more harmonies as my friends grew old,

and they were buried around me. When I finally die
I will be the most convenient ghost.

RITES

for A

You look so happy, your father will say after your first shift. You are good at being happy. You are seventeen, suddenly pretty. You understand how the world works. If you're good at school you'll meet a boy in science club or orchestra and if not you'll meet him in the parking lot. You will like him because he does not know anything about you. You'll fuck for the first time in this field if it's still a field and if by then it's a strip mall you'll go to his car. You are good at being happy with usual men, their mediocre bodies. You'll visit him at the end of his minimum wage shift as a dishwasher and his elbows will be soaked and soapy. He'll hug you and it'll leave your back cold, like the idea of wings. He'll break up with you when you both get into college out of state and you will not mourn. You will go to the DMV. You'll roll a cigarette on the sidewalk outside the DMV and light it with the lighter a girl you loved gave you for your seventeenth birthday. The girl will be named something white and usual—Susan, Alice, Emma. She will have perfect pitch or a buzzcut. She will be Asian like you. You will hate her and if you finally realize you love her she will die before you can say anything. If you do not realize you love her then you will sit on the sidewalk outside a DMV and grind your cigarette butt into the pavement, and it will pop when extinguished, like the idea of fireworks, and you will drive away, and the cigarette will outlive you.

A SELF-HELP BOOK SAYS TO CONFRONT YOUR POSSIBLE SELVES

The girl I'm supposed to be lives on a street named
for a flower   she strings ghosts up like lights   makes a border

of her body   when her fangs grow
too sharp she saws them off with a Swiss pocketknife

and does not grieve. She thanks the knife   every day
she invents new ways   to wear her body

down to shadow   I see her and every swallow
dies in my throat   midflight   and when something happens to her

her face becomes only jaw   flee   the sky
testifies; everyone   believes her. I cry on the phone. I hang

my skin up in the closet every night and scuff
my eyes in the morning and walk around smiling   and emptied.

I ask the walls if they've ever seen a ghost   like mine
they say what ghost.   What is it called

when you are given everything and still cannot be
anything? In the house where I used to live   scrawled-over Bibles

detonate in closets.   moths bash their desires
against screen doors. The girl I was supposed to be stands behind me

with the posture of a guillotine. When I hear her echo,
I close my eyes   when she calls my name

I snap her neck

GIRL, 17, HIDES FROM HER OWN SEARCH PARTY

Finally I was free to love anything I wanted.
Instead I spent weeks charting each year
of my history—back then I was beautiful, I was good,
all my friends were beautiful and good, I lived
in a narrow house where every night the ceiling
closed on me like a lid. I hid knives
in my textbooks, dreamt each night of a white table
in a muddy field, a gun on the table,
a woman holding the gun. I practiced answering her,
rehearsed my own name in the dark, still bruised,
so believe me, it wasn't a surprise to hear them years later
with floodlights, shouting my name. They said it wrong,
they always did, and on every missing poster
they'd painted my old face, so what was I to do,
in the city they made evidence? I ran,
and even cab drivers wouldn't look at me. I ran, and felt
for a fingerhold, left nail marks on the interrogation table's
wood belly. I entered through the keyhole
to a houseparty full of strangers. Racketed
through the house's narrow corridors,
a pile of knees. And every time I woke up
from the white table I woke without pain,
remembering nothing, my own name on my lips.
For months, I watched them grieve me—
now it's finally summer, my friend names her goldfish
after me, the locusts come down on the hills, turning everything
bone-white, there's an ad in the newspaper for my body

and then it's over. I am free to love anything I want. If I wasn't born
with my fear then I birthed it myself. I hate the black car
down the road. I still check every bathroom for cameras.

INHERITANCE

No one lives just once.
Get lucky and it'll be a clean break

but sometimes an earlier self lingers as you claw out
from your own sinew, she escapes to the alley on break

from the gas station night shift and grasps her name
over and over in the dark or she loses her broken

voice begging at a border or she sprints home
sure something's chasing her, breaking

brambles like the doe her neighbor shot
in the eye. *Two of these a morning, I barely break*

a sweat. I swore I could smell her, the body
sour with ghosts, blooming. Then the doe broke

through the trees again, bristling like she'd never
been killed at all. I wanted to say please break

please crumple all on your own. I wanted to say doe,
I don't want to kill you. Please, I know how to break.

//

Sister, I don't want to kill you. Please, I know how to break
my name in two. I've learned. I am mine. I am mined

for parts. Lightning. I flee past the doe, past the girl
turning porous in the field, past the sky where we whispered *mine*

mine mine because we hadn't ever seen a shaft so bright so full
of diamonds. Then the shadow I stumble into is mine,

her head bent back to her hands. She screams. I watch
her colorless tongue. I drive to the gas station where they mine

bones for neon light. I tell the cashier I like the blue. My mother's
grandmother says I'm too young for ghosts. Says mine

are mostly imagined. In the papers, officials argue Partition's murders
were a necessary cost. Progress preaches itself to me—

six bluebirds in a sack. Memory is about the body, not the past.
None of these memories are mine.

//

None of these memories are mine.
At night a small child follows me and I can't remember

what to ask. Who are your parents. How long
since your hands. Do you remember

when you're from. I watch her, praying not
for god but for language. *Child,* I swell, I remember

how to touch you, how to be a mother, how to coax
a howl to eat. I'm sorry. I said *child* and meant war. Remember

language is merely a field to walk through. Say *sky* and look, blue.
Say *escape* and find corridors of people you can't remember

you lost. Say *ghost* and you open yourself to death. A myth
and an exorcism are not different things. Remembered

in a museum: a creature, weeping. Something happened to us but
I can't remember what, I can't remember

//

I can't remember, I can't remember
anything: the gorgeous murder of country. Like quiet,

child, forget as much as you can, stop leaking
weeping streaking your ghosts across the floors. Quiet

was what the man told me before his hands
at my throat. The government wanted quiet

borders, planted graves at the aperture of progress.
When I was young, my mother took me to see a quiet

horse. I stuck my fist in its mouth. In 1947, two million people died
in migration. I fly back to the border, stand in the quiet

village again. Light on the other side of the door. It's all over
India, the parade for independence. I watch my mother get quiet

pack a bag with an old newspaper, her mother's knife, a blue dress
watch her cross the ocean and birth me again and raise me on quiet.

//

I watch her cross the ocean, birth me again, raise me on quiet:
she almost believed we were free. *Free,* say it again,

with feeling. I'm so tired of this body. I want
a new one. Don't tell me about ache, you born all over again

in your ancestors' sludge. Some of us learned to speak
in a cemetery or a dark kitchen, practiced again and again

to twist our mouths around our names. Some of us emerge
into ghosts so silent only the silence is left. Again,

my people die. Again, I swallow, reach back. Cussing cusping
homesick beast. Hey, what's your name again.

I want to be called sky. Or bite. Palm. Air. I want
to shatter my name so no one can call for me ever again—

so my ghosts lose their way. Please, give me something useful
to do with my dead. Please: the words shot limp, gone, again

//

My dead—please—the words shot limp, gone. Again,
I make it summer because what else is there to want

except escape, banged-up Volvo whirring past preachers
promising hell, past my grandmother's mother who wanted

to be a poet, past the year my mother lived below the temple believed
nothing and all the moonlight spilled over, past the want

for ancestors or a good story or a body—and time unspools
again. The border has my mother's eyes. It wants

my body useful. Wants me thankful, silent,
leaving on a winning streak. I don't want

to be a happy corpse. I turn on the tap, scrub at my skin
and watch the water turn red like a wanted

poster. Not even my grief is new. I wander through corridors
where the dead are everywhere and full of want.

//

Where the dead are everywhere and full of want.
Where you can leap between centuries and not once

glimpse the faces of kin. Where every footfall leaves
wounds in the ash. I want to prove we were here once.

Everyone I could be is dead. I want someone to call
my name, to swear my body had been new once.

The gas station says enlist if you're devoted to your country
and I forget which. God of neon signs or dead women dear god o
    god once

I believed. Once, a girl let ghosts into her body, brushed their hair
with her antlers, and she was never lonely again. Once,

a god was anything you couldn't see up close. I promise—
I will kneel into the brush, try to stand, just once.

Leave the porch light on for my ancestors.
No one lives just once.

BABY GIRL'S THIRD BIRTHDAY

In a dream, the end came. It had my mother's eyes. Everyone was flying except for me. I looked up and saw wind in their skirts. It was raining. I was wearing a green dress. I turned off the sun. Go you! screamed the woman. I ran up the slide and didn't slide down. I climbed a tree and watched the boy smile with his braces wide like big harps. Once my eyes didn't let me open. Harps are scary. Everyone floated up to the moon and I couldn't fly. I dug a small hole in the sandbox and stuck my hand in it. How long will I be drowning, I asked aloud. I was wearing big red lips. Up! Up! smiled my mother. A man put his hands on my face to see if I was bright. I like rabbits when they're alive. I want to kill the moon. I beg the dream to let me back into my body.

INSIDE EVERY POEM YOU CAN HEAR MUFFLED SCREAMS

I like to eat my shadow. I like
to stick my hand out the window and choke

the first bird that flies by until it turns flimsy
in my fist, melts dead to the ground. I like birds.

I steal my ancestors' ghosts from clotheslines
and wave them as if they're sudden flags. I don't

remember why. I invent yet another universe
where I am hunted to great applause.

Someone else dies and it must be
a poem. Maybe with blood. Maybe

screams. Maybe a mother and child
at a dining table, and the child is wailing,

but you never see their hands. I like to stand
outside my body and set her on fire.

Watch her wrap her thumbs around her throat
break skin, but barely. I wonder

if the dead know we are writing about them.
I wonder if the missing girl wanted

to be a symbol. I worry that to be a poet
is to sit and wait for beautiful things

to die. To exploit distance. To steal
flight. To wring murder into myth, to retell it—

PARABLE OF THE UNCLEAN LAND

And then every animal we'd ever slain clamored forth,
moaning like men, moaning like deer, the bullet
still in them, the bullet still rushing forward,
and there we were, steeped in blood. We'd been deadly,
we'd had to be—two women alone in the backwater
in my father's old house and her father's borrowed shoes.
We were hungry, we were always hungry,
so I tracked blood into the house, hid a .45 in the closet,
dressed to mourn. My father taught me how
to kill a thing and not flinch. First of four brothers
to skin veal, first to shoot a deer in the eye.
His wife was the woman at the fire who turned
his creatures on her spit. I was the girl. I watched
the way he held his gun, stayed up to practice
on the plywood out back. And when I told my father
I loved a woman he hit me in the jaw,
stayed up all night shooting plywood while I watched
from my window, and the next morning I made him breakfast.
I smiled, told him *yes sir I understand sir I am just learning
how to be a proper woman sir*, followed the rats
into the smallest corners and felt dead
for years after. Unlike him, I am a good man;
every time I kill, I bury it. When he died I lived in his house,
killed deer the way he did, kissed the woman he hated,
kept goldfish. The house yawned open, and we had to try,
for the last time, to not die here. We fled
to the train station. Fruit flies hissed at the ticket counter,

covered the welcome sign. One deer's left eye was winched shut,
angry purple. Hissing, the goldfish appeared at my feet,
dirt still scattered on its flank, the shallows
of a grave. I was so sure that in the new city,
in the new house, I would be able to love her.
The creatures stood in a crescent, stamping their oily feet,
and we stood apart from one another with our eyes open.

BEARINGS

You are in control of your life, you are
in control of your life, you are in control
of your life. Fine. I'm all heat, all panting

witness. Leaking, weeping sweat
through my scales. A thrum of minnows circles me
for seventy days. I turn light-hungry, turn blue

and desperate for chocolate or blood,
turn in my sleep toward the carcasses
of sinking turtles, silver fishing wire

strung welted through their mouths. You
are in control of your life, says the fish
before his flank snaps up to the light,

dead already. I blink and forget him.
I hate the water for making me tell the truth
about my life. Hate the people above for celebrating

my new ghosthood, for looking down
and down into the water and seeing something
like a god. Someday there'll be nothing left to spare.

AN EDITOR SAYS CAN YOU PUT MORE FOREIGN WORDS IN YOUR POEMS

A white man shouts *you write just*
like this other brown girl poet I know,
do you know her? I don't. I do,

she is me, I am her, we stand on a stage
and sob and at the end everyone claps
and says we're strong. She rides home

on the subway and considers the news.
Then, in front of her apartment, she cries
about her *immigrant parents,* then plants

a tree native to her country. That's the story
you like, isn't it? I'll give you this. In my most
evolved form, when I'm angry, it's only

the pretty kind. I'm never caught
without makeup, a grateful smile, a quote
from the other poet of color you read

this year. At a reading, a white woman says
you only write about heritage. I want to say, *no,*
I write about kitchens better than church, secret

glances, cameras, but instead I blush. I am grateful
to be here. I am grateful to be heard. And they love me,
or they say they do. I don a white dress and fly

through the market, screaming a poem. At the end
of the reading, I say *thank you,* thank you,
for correcting my armor. Thank you, for slicing

my speech into only sobs. All this time,
I've written my ache for you.
All this time, I have been yours.

HOPSCOTCH

I was a god like any other, startled
by my hands, poised to spring. Landed on the edge

of seven, elbows inscribing pavement,
my shoelaces unraveling. I stole curse words from the boys,

slipped them between hops on the street
that looked like a postcard with the back blank,

shutters claimed by daisies. In Ohio all my favorite birds
died of blunt force trauma against glass doors. The good men

wore white shirts and choked the cleanest women
in the sedan to church. We played hopscotch, played

until our scraped knees hurt worse than the whistle
of a switch, worse than the thwack of firewood,

worse than our torn hides in the basement,
breathing. The teacher kept rulers sharp

in her desk, warm for our knuckles. We snuck chalk
to paint the game out back, drew footprints

like weapons. How long ago was it
that I realized this town would never love me back? Girls

went into alleys and did not come out. Girls went
into churches and did not come out and I was not scared,

more quiet. Hopscotching to the next year, the sun spinning
like a turntable. And we prayed, but only to the physical,

the switch, the boys in empty stadiums, the men
who took us out behind the shed

wielding wood they cut themselves, oh,
they were good men, almost worthy gods,

damned if they'd ever let a girl talk back.

PRODIGY

Alice was better than all of us,
the ache of it coming up white-hot

when she won an audition or booked front page
on county news, everyone testifying that yes,

we knew her, this town would be nothing
without her god that girl

she was really something. She played violin,
alone in the big house with the floral wallpaper

and gold-framed Bible quotes where God preached Himself
like a sparrow in heat. I hid how I watched her,

her bone fist, her misaligned jaw. She peeled glue
from her fingers, punched her old man in the teeth, limped onto stage

like an ugly cat. And when she spun her car
into the lake we mourned only the myth of her,

playing Wagner, not smiling. Or Alice dancing
in clothes she stole from her father, stumbling

into the kitchen, some rock number on the radio
like the stale roar of his Buick, knuckling her down

and down into the passenger seat, her violin knocking in the trunk
on the way to a concert. Her father all dime-store reverent

when she played solo, quiet when she finished,
the audience rising into prayers for daughters like her.

PINE STREET

There's a game we used to play called Mercy:
someone twisted your arm back so tendons almost volted

through skin. The boy whispered in my ear *call mercy,*
you know you're just a girl, I'll stop if you call, just

do it. I fought gasps until everyone else surrendered
to the sidewalk, until a scream swelled through

my throat, until streetlights smeared
into dropped dimes. I swear, I waited the longest

of anyone. Eight years later, an old woman
on the same street said *you're so strong, I don't know*

how you do it. Cupped her hands on my forehead,
passed them through my translucent form as if to give

a blessing, her breath rising sour into my mouth. I was admired,
though I was not loved. An image of a girl

but never the girl. The holy men said *your life is a battle*
you win through prayer, amen, and the entire pew stood

as if to attention, cheers bleeding outward. I could never
leave that street. And when all the poplars shriveled up

I painted them forest green. I hid my gentleness like a wound,
and so, when I glimpsed something—a deer?—flashing

through those wooded backyards, those tiny metallic sparks,
of course I assumed it had to be a dagger.

What wouldn't you believe to be victorious? I mean
alive. I scurried off into the smallest burrows to fight

alone, orphaned myself and called it liberation, left
my body at the altar of anything that flinched. The dirt

liked blood, and I learned it. Returned on my knees,
studied how to hold a shout, my arms

unhinging. Watched as I was buried, the dark
so full of writhe, a knife sutured to my throat,

something weak in me beginning, generously, to cry.

PERFORMANCE REVIEW

Two blocks from us someone robs a bank
in a gas mask then runs away to his top-floor
precipice, kisses his boyfriend and says babe,

I won it big. They buy dinner from Subway
and sit outside the fluorescent drugstore
knees touching, melting into each other

like stalactites. I know what he's escaping:
this town, these billboards where God preaches
Himself like a sparrow in heat. At my boss's party,

I console the railing and listen to the metal band beg
from the apartment below. I waste the morning
scrolling Twitter and death records from when my friends

were alive and top listings on Craigslist:
cover photo of a pretty girl cross-legged on the hood
of a Chevy, keys glinting in her teeth. The man trapped

in the radio says this is gonna be the best year yet.
I've become a big self-care person lately, I tell my boss.
I keep bones in my office next to the plaques I've won

for being a good hatchet. I always email back.
I watch the bank robber flee from my office window
and think *take the money go run run run.*

GHOST TOWN, OHIO

Anything can be a spinning tire or anything can be a dead end
speckled with spit or anything can be a memorial
if you look hard enough. So I name this town, the hunger

of its dogs. I search for scuff marks on the statues,
take them as evidence of the living. Hear the rain against
an abandoned roof and think of the water

on my father's hands ten years ago, his head bent in the sink
after a day at the hospital, scrubbing and scrubbing
until his skin dissolved. Like him,

I enter the horizon and promise to keep quiet. I circle
the map where my parents grew up, circle the town begging
for someone to reply. I bless the doe sleeping on the road

before I see she's full of bullets. I whisper my name
in a church and call the echo my ancestor, angel
smacking her lips on the hard syllables. The dogs bark

but do not get up to beg. My father gave me
the posture of a guillotine, ready always
for the war years. I have an accent

in every language. This town doesn't remember
it was once a town. My father on the phone
wants to know what I'm looking for.

ACKNOWLEDGMENTS

I'm so grateful to the editors of the following anthologies and print and online journals for making a home for my work:

Palette Poetry: "Heaven"
Counterclock (as part of the PATCHWORK film-poetry initiative): "Simple Machines"
DIALOGIST: "A Self-Help Book Says to Confront Your Possible Selves"
GASHER: "Girl, 17, Hides from Her Own Search Party"
Post Road: "Prodigy"
THRUSH: "Parable of the Unclean Land"
Split Lip Magazine: "Pine Street"
Kenyon Review: "Ghost Town, Ohio"

To Saniya, Karsten, and Aria—you are my lodestars. I love you, I love you, I love you. There are no other words.

To Kit Frick, Diane Goettel, and the Black Lawrence Press team— thank you for your care with this project. I couldn't have imagined a better team to bring this chapbook into being, and I'm so happy to be part of BLP's lineage. I'm so grateful we got to work together.

To Claudia Cortese—you were one of the first writers I loved, and then my first real mentor. You showed me what it was to be wholly your own. Thank you for getting it.

To Malvika Jolly—meeting you made me realize the project of my life. Thank you for your tenderness and vision, and for all the heart you put into making our little community feel corporeal. I can't wait to see you again.

To Annelyse Gelman—you're a brilliant writer and friend, and I keep your words with me everywhere I go. Thank you for everything. I'm so proud to know you.

To Danie Shokoohi—thank you for making your living room a poetry salon, for slipping the most perfect books into my bag, for understanding exactly what this book was hungry for.

To Linda Tirado—thank you for always knowing. Thank you for taking a Greyhound for me, for all the oranges, for always reminding me I'm bold. Tim Minchin will forever be a staple. I love you. There's nowhere I'd rather be from.

To everyone who's spent years running—I hope it won't be much longer. I hope you find somewhere that sees you. I promise, you already know how.

GAIA RAJAN is the author of the chapbooks *Moth Funerals* (Glass Poetry Press, 2020) and *Killing It* (Black Lawrence Press, 2022). Her work is published or forthcoming in the 2022 Best of the Net anthology, *The Kenyon Review*, *THRUSH*, *Split Lip Magazine*, *diode*, *Palette Poetry*, and elsewhere. Gaia is an intern at Poets House, journal editor for *Half Mystic*, and web manager for *Honey Literary*. You can find her online at gaiarajan.com and @gaiarajan on Twitter and Instagram.